the best of *ideals*

Throughout the years our readers have written and suggested that we combine past offerings from our magazine into a single edition. In response to your suggestions we published the Best of Ideals in January of 1977. Your acceptance was most gratifying and as a result we are proud to present another, more recent collection of Ideals best-loved poetry, prose, photographs, and artwork from the last ten years. We have included for your pleasure the finest variety of inspirational, poetic, nostalgic, philosophical, holiday, and seasonal material. The tremendous color quality will bring the Ideals experience to life for you. We hope you enjoy each page as much as we enjoy sharing this with you.

compiled by
Jan Frances Engel

Editorial Director, James Kuse
Managing Editor, Ralph Luedtke
Photographic Editor, Gerald Koser

ISBN 0-89542-001-5 395

For each and every joyful thing,
For twilight swallows on the wing,
For all that nests and all that sings,

For fountains cool that laugh and leap,
For rivers running to the deep,
For happy, care-forgetting sleep,

For stars that pierce the somber dark,
For morn, awaking with the lark,
For life new-stirring neath the bark,

For sunshine and the blessed rain,
For budding grove and blossoming lane,
For the sweet silence of the plain,

For bounty springing from the sod,
For every step by beauty trod,
For each dear gift of joy, thank God!

Florence Earle Coates

CONTENTS

pring

Blessed are the poor in spirit: for theirs is the kingdom of heaven.

Blessed are they that mourn: for they shall be comforted.

Blessed are the meek: for they shall inherit the earth.

Blessed are they which do hunger and thirst after righteousness: for they shall be filled.

Blessed are the merciful: for they shall obtain mercy.

Blessed are the pure in heart: for they shall see God.

Blessed are the peacemakers: for they shall be called the children of God.

Blessed are they which are persecuted for righteousness' sake: for theirs is the kingdom of heaven.

Blessed are ye, when men shall revile you, and persecute you, and shall say all manner of evil against you falsely, for my sake.

Rejoice, and be exceeding glad: for great is your reward in heaven.

Matthew 5: 3-12

Nature's Garden

Patience Strong

The fields are like a patchwork quilt
   of colours rich and gay . . .
Beautiful they look upon
   this sunny summer day.
Crimson sorrel, purple clover,
   daisies gold and white,
Meadowsweet and buttercups
   and poppies bold and bright.

Thickly grow the tangled flowers
   along the river's edge,
Sweetly twine the roses
   through the lattice of the hedge . . .
Speedwell, bindweed,
   periwinkle and anemone
Glowing in the grasses
   like a living tapestry.

City parks and country gardens
   in the golden days
Please the eye with formal beds
   and borders all ablaze.
Lovely are the flowers round cottage door
   and stately hall,
But nature's own wild garden
   is the loveliest of all.

The Easter Story

Alinari-Scala

*V*erily, verily, I say unto you,
That ye shall weep and lament,
but the world shall rejoice; and
ye shall be sorrowful, but your
sorrow shall be turned into joy.

St. John 16:20

From Nazareth He Comes

From Nazareth He comes, the carpenter
Who knows of hammering and blows that break
The worker's hands. From Galilee He comes,
The fisherman who walks upon the lake.

Through fields of harvest, ripe for plucking grain,
Along the dusty roads that go beside
The vineyards, Christ, the noble carpenter,
Goes to the city to be crucified.

Jerusalem's streets are filled with those
Who cry "Hosanna!" and others, "Crucify!"
For all of these He hangs upon the cross
That lifts itself into the purple sky.

For all of these the Master lived and died . . .
His lamp is tall and bright; our lamps are dim,
But we can see the way ahead of us,
For where the Master goes we go with Him.

Raymond Kresensky

Not in the silence only,
Nor in the solitude,
Let my thoughts rise to
Thee in praise,
My God, so great, so good.
But mid the din and noise
Of city conflict rude;
In crowded street where
    daily pours
The hurrying multitude.
Not on the Sabbath only,
In the dear house of prayer,
Where earthly din
    cannot intrude,
And only God is there.
But all week long, in spite
Of care and vanity;
That thus, even in the crowd,
    I may
Be still alone with Thee.

Horatius Bonar
1808-1889

O heavenly Father, who hast filled the
world with beauty: Open, we beseech
Thee, our eyes to behold thy gracious
hand in all thy works, that rejoicing
in thy whole creation, we may learn to
serve Thee with gladness; for the sake
of Him through whom all things were
made, thy Son Jesus Christ our Lord.

Book of Common Prayer (USA)

Grant me, O Lord, the royalty of in-
ward happiness, and the serenity which
comes from living close to Thee. Daily
renew in me the sense of joy, and let
the eternal spirit of the Father dwell
in my soul and body, filling every
corner of my heart with light and
grace, so that, bearing about with me
the infection of a good courage, I may
be a diffuser of life, and may meet all
ills and cross accidents with gallant
and high-hearted courage, giving Thee
thanks always for all things. Amen.

Author Unknown

To Awaken Each Morning

Thomas Dekker

To awaken each morning with a smile brightening
my face . . .

To greet the day with reverence for the oppor-
tunities it contains . . .

To approach my work with a clean mind . . .

To hold ever before me, even in the doing of
little things, the ultimate purpose towards
which I am working . . .

To meet men and women with laughter on my lips
and love in my heart . . .

To be gentle, kind and courteous through all
the hours . . .

To approach the night with weariness that ever
woos sleep and the joy that comes from work
well-done . . .

This is how I desire to waste wisely my days.

April Showers

Oh, the showers of April are beautiful things,
  When the sun shines through and a robin sings;
The glittering drops come dashing by,
  Eager to leave the restless sky,
And drop on the old earth's welcoming lap,
  As the flowers awake from their winter nap,
And peep from their cover, soft and brown,
  To smile as the rain comes tumbling down.

Then the dull ground changes to living green,
  And hints of the abundance of life are seen;
When the sun comes through, and a robin sings,
  Oh, the showers of April are wonderful things!

Martha Hood

Spring Rain

Like a cooling kiss from heaven
  A sweet, descending shower,
Falls gently on the buds
  Of bush and tree and flower.

It bades them to awaken
  And blossom forth again,
As spring in all her splendor
  Comes tripping down the lane.

Each silver, shining raindrop
  Has a wondrous tale to tell,
As they fall on every garden,
  The woodlands and each dell.

Then as the raindrops cease
  And the golden sun rides high,
A vivid, brilliant rainbow
  Appears from out the sky.

'Tis the farewell of the raindrops
  Bidding earth a fond adieu,
Until they come to fall again
  And refresh the earth anew.

LaVerne P. Larson

Faith of a Farmer

A farmer understands deep certainties,
Knows winter is a doorway to the spring,
Walks quiet aisles of prayer where templed trees
Prove resurrection of each living thing.

Steadfast he turns fresh furrows to the sun
And feels new sunlight on his old, old fields;
Each drop of dew and rain an orison
Of hope to guarantee his harvest yields.

He bares his head against an April sky,
Sure of the constant greening of the grass;
When seedlings sprout he does not question why,
Hears trust in wild geese calling as they pass.

A farmer's faith affirms an Easter name
When spring returns a green and living flame.

Helen Virden

The Tale of Peter Rabbit

Beatrix Potter

Once upon a time there were four little rabbits, and their names were Flopsy, Mopsy, Cottontail and Peter.

They lived with their mother in a sandbank, underneath the root of a very big fir tree.

"Now, my dears," said old Mrs. Rabbit one morning, "you may go into the fields or down the lane, but don't go into Mr. McGregor's garden: your father met with an accident there; he was put in a pie by Mrs. McGregor. Now run along, and don't get into mischief. I am going out."

Then old Mrs. Rabbit took a basket and her umbrella, and went through the woods to the baker's. She bought a loaf of bread and five currant buns.

Flopsy, Mopsy and Cottontail, who were good little bunnies, went down the lane to gather blackberries; but Peter, who was very naughty, ran straight away to Mr. McGregor's garden, and squeezed under the gate! First he ate some lettuces and some French beans; and then he ate some radishes; and then, feeling rather sick, he went to look for some parsley.

But round the end of a cucumber frame, whom should he meet but Mr. McGregor.

Mr. McGregor was on his hands and knees planting out young cabbages, but he jumped up and ran after Peter, waving a rake and calling out, "Stop thief!"

Peter was most dreadfully frightened; he rushed all over the garden, for he had forgotten the way back to the gate. He lost one of his shoes among the cabbages, and the other shoe amongst the potatoes.

After losing them, he ran on four legs, and went faster, so that I think he might have gotten away altogether, if he had not unfortunately run into a gooseberry net, and got caught by the large buttons on his jacket. It was a blue jacket with brass buttons, quite new.

Peter gave himself up for lost, and shed big tears; but his sobs were overheard by some friendly sparrows, who flew to him in great excitement, and implored him to exert himself.

Continued

Mr. McGregor came up with a sieve, which he intended to pop upon the top of Peter; but Peter wriggled out just in time, leaving his jacket behind him.

He rushed into the toolshed, and jumped into a can. It would have been a beautiful thing to hide in, if it had not had so much water in it.

Mr. McGregor was quite sure that Peter was somewhere in the toolshed, perhaps hidden underneath a flowerpot. He began to turn them over carefully, looking under each.

Presently Peter sneezed — "Kertyschoo!" Mr. McGregor was after him in no time, and tried to put his foot upon Peter, who jumped out the window, upsetting three plants. The window was too small for Mr. McGregor, and he was tired of running after Peter. He went back to his work.

Peter sat down to rest; he was out of breath and trembling with fright, and he had not the least idea which way to go. Also he was very damp with sitting in that can.

After a time he began to wander about, going lippity-lippity not very fast, and looking all around.

He found a door in a wall; but it was locked, and there was no room for a fat little rabbit to squeeze underneath.

An old mouse was running in and out over the stone doorstep, carrying peas and beans to her family in the wood. Peter asked her the way to the gate, but she had such a large pea in her mouth that she could not answer. She only shook her head at him. Peter began to cry.

Then he tried to find his way straight across the garden, but he became more and more puzzled. Presently he came to a pond where Mr. McGregor filled his watercans. A white cat was staring at some goldfish; she sat very, very still, but now and then, the tip of her tail twitched as if it were alive. Peter thought it best to go away without speaking to her; he had heard about cats from his cousin, little Benjamin Bunny.

He went back toward the toolshed, but suddenly, quite close to him, he heard the noise of a hoe — scr-r-ritch, scratch, scratch, scritch. Peter scuttered underneath the bushes. But presently, as nothing happened, he came out, and climbed upon a wheelbarrow and peeped over. The first thing that he saw was Mr. McGregor hoeing onions. His back was turned toward Peter, and beyond him was the gate.

Peter got down very quietly off the wheelbarrow, and started running as fast as he could go, along a straight walk behind some black currant bushes.

Mr. McGregor caught sight of him at the corner, but Peter did not care. He slipped underneath the gate, and was safe at last in the woods outside the garden.

Mr. McGregor hung up the little jacket and the shoes for a scarecrow to frighten the blackbirds.

Peter never stopped running or looked behind him till he got home to the big fir tree.

He was so tired that he flopped down upon the nice soft sand on the floor of the rabbit hole and shut his eyes. His mother was busy cooking; she wondered what he had done with his clothes. It was the second little jacket and pair of shoes that Peter had lost in a fortnight!

I am sorry to say that Peter was not very well during the evening.

His mother put him to bed, and made some camomile tea; and she gave a dose of it to Peter!

"One tablespoonful to be taken at bedtime."

But Flopsy, Mopsy and Cottontail had bread and milk and blackberries for supper.

I Want a Pasture

I want a pasture for next door neighbor;
    The sea to be just across the way.
I want to stand at my door for hours,
    Talking and passing the time of day
Unhurried, as country people do
Season on season, a whole year through.

I want to give greeting to frost and sun;
    To gossip with thunder and tides and bees;
To mark the doing of wind in boughs;
    Watch apples redden on crooked trees.
I want to hail each passing thing
That moves, fleet-footed, by fin, or wing.

I want far islands to grow familiar
    As neighbors' faces; clouds be more plain
Than granite boulder, than web of spider
    Patterned with intricate drops of rain.
I want to be wise as the oldest star,
Young as the waves and grasses are.

Rachel Field

Spring on the Farm

The rich brown earth yields to the farmer's plowshare.
The fertile field in graceful furrows lies.
A mourning dove croons sadly from the meadow
While overhead a graceful sea gull cries.

Along the southern border of the garden
Young tender shoots are bursting through the sod.
Roots, seeds and bulbs that lay in winter's bosom,
With life renewed look up to greet their God.

Out in the pasture lot along the creek-bed
Where turf is soft and willows gently sway,
A newborn colt staggers beside its mother
And sweet-faced lambs frisk gaily at their play.

The haymow harbors tiny tumbling kittens;
A mother hen struts with her yellow brood.
A curious puppy, wandering from the litter
A lovely monarch butterfly pursues.

The fragrance of the dew-drenched lawns at dawning,
The singing hills and warm contented days;
The blooming meadow smiles through fragrant blossoms
As mother nature sings her psalm of praise.

Marion Olson

You Can Hear Music Everywhere

Ruth Barker

You can hear music everywhere
If you have a heart that sings;
You can hear a melody
In ordinary things . . .

In the whisper of the wind
Through the branches of the trees,
In the chirping of the crickets,
In the humming of the bees,
In the chatter of the squirrel,
In the whir of tiny wings . . .
You can hear music everywhere
If you have a heart that sings.

In the rhythm of the raindrops,
In the rippling of a stream,
In the lilt of children's laughter
As they romp upon the green,
In the warm voice of a friend
And the comfort that it brings . . .
You can hear music everywhere
If you have a heart that sings.

©

In the Forest

Helen Prodoehl

I walked into the forest
And I knew that God was there,
I needed no cathedral
To remind me of His care.

This was His sanctuary
Where peace and quiet reigned:
And as I walked the forest,
Tranquillity I gained.

I heard God's choir singing
A song so loud and clear;
It was just a songbird chorus
But it sounded so sincere.

I guess the birds all felt that
Our God was very near,
And in the forest temple
Their song of praise He'd hear.

©

25

It's Easter Again

It's the time of renewal beginning again:
Great clumps of violets purple the lane.

There's a change in the landscape wherever you look.
The duck takes her brood for a swim in the brook.

Alice Leedy Mason

Little Downy Things

Something new to sound and sight
Has happened almost overnight

And man must move with constant care
For downy things are everywhere.

Pussywillows, soft and round,
Have dressed the willow tree with down.

Squirrels scampering through the trees
Are scolding very noisily.

Baby rabbits venture out
Beside the broken waterspout.

In the pasture on the lea
The lambs all frolic merrily.

Baby chicks like balls of string
Have gathered neath their mother's wing.

Kittens think it's loads of fun
Chasing beetles in the sun.

A bee beside a buttercup
Challenges a frisky pup.

Ducklings love the countryside
With tall green grass where they can hide

Or swim the brook with such a flair
Like balls of fluff just floating there.

The heart awakens, new at last,
To find the winter gloom is past . . .

Because the Easter season brings
A host of little downy things.

Alice Leedy Mason

27

THE BIRDS

There is a timeless quality about the birds
That comforts me, when all about me I see change.
And sometimes in the changes, so swift they are,
   so fearful,
I would forget that underneath are still the laws
   of God.
But I am brought again to sense the sure foundation,
When in their appointed time the birds come back
   in spring.
When all these fields were only prairie land and forest,
Before the plows broke up the sod and cattle grazed,
Still was the killdeer's call, the plaintive,
   haunting measure
That I hear now across the marsh, when evening comes.

There is no change! The swallow still is grace incarnate;
The flicker still beats out his snare drum, loud tattoo;
The oriole is flash of flame in Maytime's greening . . .
Among the young oak leaves, the jay's a brilliant blue.

I do not need to wonder what hues, what feathered patterns
Clothed them in centuries past. I know, unchanged, unchanging,
Each generation, brief though it may be, repeats
Once more the timeless laws, the pattern for its species.
In years to come, my children's children, standing here,
Where I have stood, may see a vastly different scene.
Gone, perhaps, this lane of maple trees, this wood;
Gone all the things, perhaps, that make it home to me.
But there will be a link, the same swift flight
   of swallows . . .
The same bright flash of orioles' wings, the
   killdeer's call.

Wilma Black

Summer

Come Walk With Me

Kay Hillyard

Come walk with me
To trace the route
Our cherished water takes
From source to sea.

Let's go to high country first
To watch the water tumble
From the top of rugged cliffs
To rocks, worn smooth, below.
Let's enjoy the mist upon our faces
As we listen to the roar
Of the swirling water
As it rushes on its way.

Then comes a sudden calmness
As the water branches out,
And quietly wanders here and there
Around large granite boulders,
Forming clear reflecting pools
That mirror sun and shadow
Throughout most of the day.

Now, since the route to sea
Is never constant
But widens and narrows
As Mother Nature orders,
We watch that same water rush
Between some ancient rocks—
Moving with such force that
It looks like fine spun glass,
Before it settles down to form
Another quiet-looking pool.

From that unruffled pool
A tiny portion slips away
To make a bubbling little brook
That dances past tall grasses
And looks as if it's laughing
As it tickles well-aged rocks.

Inevitably, all streams and brooks
Will meet to form
A broad bright ribbon
Of ever-moving water
That laps at grassy banks
And curls around low branches—
A river that's most sensitive
To wind and man-made obstacles
As it gently flows toward home.

And now it's time
For you and me
To make a solemn pledge
To try to keep that water clean
From mountain source to sea.

From HARVEST YEARS, June 1971
Used by permission of the author

A Child
Is Someone
to Love

A child is someone who...

eats pickles and peanut butter and chocolate, all together.

likes to hear your songs, even if you can't sing.

starts Thanksgiving dinner by asking, "What's for dessert?"

holds your hand and trusts you.

dances to music inside his head.

thinks wire clothes hangers were meant for bending into interesting shapes.

knows right away whether you like him and he likes you.

is more in awe of someone two years older than of someone twenty years older.

knows the only reason for eating breakfast cereals is to get the box tops.

is afraid of the dark and not ashamed to say so.

enjoys helping you, especially when you don't need any help.

wants to be an actor on Monday and a teacher on Tuesday. By Wednesday, he has decided he will be an actor who teaches and is also a cowboy.

comes and kisses you and curls up in your lap when you are sad.

loves you for no particular reason except that you just happen to be you.

knows whether there's love in a home.

mixes milk, coke, ginger ale, mustard, ketchup, sugar, and salt . . . then asks if you'd like to taste it.

can hardly wait until his next birthday.

begins to explain a situation by telling you, "It wasn't my fault, but . . ."

has trouble taking "No" for an answer.

is in search of a comfortable lap.

knows how to enjoy God's little creatures . . . bugs and beetles and worms.

plants a seed today and is disappointed when tomorrow comes and there is no flower.

is scared by too much neatness.

thinks you're great, unless you go out of your way to prove you aren't.

knows that peanut butter and jelly tastes better than caviar.

can cry when he's hurt.

Berna Rauch

Sea Town

Frances Frost

This is a salt steep-cobbled town
   where every morning the men go down
   to breathe the sun-wet sea;

where maples shadow the sloping street
   and the dawn-cool reek of fog is sweet
   in the dooryard chestnut tree.

This is the place where fishermen
   stride down to the silver wharves again,
   to the creak of the waiting hulls

where a lifting leeward wind comes through
   and a shaking sail with a patch or two
   is followed by flashing gulls.

This is a small brine-weathered town
   where the houses lean to winds gone down
   the other side of the world,

where chimney-smoke floats blue to gray,
   piling that creaks with ended day
   while the snagging ropes are hurled.

This is the place where fishermen
   stride up the cobbled hill again
   and scan the faint-starred skies,

where doors stand open to lilac-shine
   and supper-drift blows warm and fine
   and windows have seaward eyes.

Summer Soliloquy

Summer's come on kitten feet;
Gentle breezes blowing
Like little kitten sighs.
Pensive cat, you are
So languid, still . . .
Revelling in the summer sun
As the world sings round you.

Happy bird sounds filter
Through lacy garments green—
Bees in quick, ambitious flight,
Their phantom wings abuzz,
Seek scented flowers bright.

Velvet pansies, alive, aglow,
Are little people faces
Nodding, bobbing,
Sharing summer secrets.

Azure skies, sailboat clouds
Drifting, billowing
In graceful harmony;
Soft as a butterfly's
Gossamer wings.

Stay, pensive cat,
Sink into summer.
Life is this honey-sweet day,
Tranquil and free,
Just right for dreaming.

Joan Callahan

GOLDEN HOURS OF SUMMER

Where summer basks 'neath peaceful skies
The spell of perfect weather lies,
Bright meadow flowers congregate
Where raucous starlings hold debate
And sheep in pastures graze serene
Beside stone walls where bluejays preen.
The children spend each sunny day
In games that small fry love to play.

The bright days stretch in lazy ease
Beneath the shade of willow trees,
Where busy insects toil to hoard
The winter fare lush fields afford.
They have no time for pleasure's lure;
They first must winter's stores assure,
But elsewhere in the world of sun
The main concern is having fun.

Summer lives briefly, rich and well,
To lavish charm in vale and dell.
She's not concerned with somber ways;
She lives to savor carefree days.
Her flowered mantle spreads the scent
Of perfumed days in gladness spent.
She brings the land the gentle spell
Of golden hours when all is well.

Brian F. King

The Sunshine Shop

The sunshine shop is stocked with every kind of sun,
With happiness and bliss and gladness and plain fun.
You take your choice; and as for payment, why, it's free!
This sunshine selling is as simple as can be!
You just take all the sunshine you can carry,
And no one asks for payment when you go.
The sunshine shop is just around some corner—
Perhaps this corner here—you never know!

Mary Carolyn Davies

Laughter

Laughter is release, and so
Let laughter have its way;
We grown folk need our laughter
As children need their play.

Laughter is as precious as
The gold we ever seek;
It clears the brain of misty clouds;
It is tonic to the weak.

Laughter is a beauty aid;
It smooths out lines of care.
Add laughter to your daily "must"
Of work and food and prayer.

Olive Lair Smith

The Majesty of Trees

There is a serene and settled majesty in woodland scenery that enters into the soul, and delights and elevates it, and fills it with noble inclinations. As the leaves of trees are said to absorb all noxious qualities of the air and to breathe forth a purer atmosphere, so it seems to me as if they drew from us all sordid and angry passions, and breathed forth peace and philanthropy.

There is something nobly simple and pure in a taste for the cultivation of forest trees. It argues, I think, a sweet and generous nature to have this strong relish for the beauties of vegetation and this friendship for the hardy and glorious sons of the forest. There is a grandeur of thought connected with this part of rural economy. It is, if I may be allowed the figure, the heroic line of husbandry. It is worthy of liberal, and free-born, and aspiring men. He who plants an oak, looks forward to future ages, and plants for posterity. Nothing can be less selfish than this.

Washington Irving

Sheep Pastures

Out of the noise and clamor of the town,
I have come down
To this green pasture land where sheep
Graze in the golden light,
Where shadows creep,
As deliberately as they, across the grass.
The slow hours pass,
And I am one with the rhythm and the rhyme
Of this still land, this quiet time;
Even my hurrying heart has stayed its pace
Within this quiet place.

Time is nothing here—the sun, the moon,
Come neither late nor soon;
There is no change in the ways of sheep.
They have kept step with the ages,
Hurrying not at all, and no relentless call
Bids them keep appointment with the hours.
If I could stay day after day
Here in this clean green land, perhaps I, too,
Could be more true to the movement of the years;
Could march with time until the far sublime
Music of the spheres would reach my ears,
And I could keep the tempo my life through
That sheep and shepherds do.

Grace Noll Crowell

Summer in the Country

O it's summer in the country;
　　And at breaking of the dawn,
There are visions of enchantment
　　Like petunias on the lawn.

O'er the split-rail fences climbing
　　Are the roses red and white,
And the dew upon their petals
　　Make it such a splendid sight.

The great house and barn are sprawling
　　Underneath a morning sky,
And the song of bright red robins
　　Is heard in trees nearby.

There are sounds within the barnyard;
　　Animals are stirring now;
Roosters lustily are crowing;
　　What these lovely scenes endow!

It is summer in the country;
　　And as day dawns fair and bright,
I but marvel at the wonders
　　That transpired overnight.

Georgia B. Adams

Rural Life Has Charm

Rural life is for living;
The days are zestful and long . . .
You greet the sun at dawning
And the day begins with song.

The rolling hills are friendly;
Meadow grass lush and green.
A star-spangled sky above you,
So fragrant the air and clean.

You sow and reap in season
And God rewards you in kind.
You're one with all things around you . . .
Sweet peace fills body and mind.

Eleanor Fiock

A thing of beauty is a joy forever:
Its loveliness increases; it will never

Pass into nothingness; but still will keep
A bower quiet for us, and a sleep

Full of sweet dreams, and health, and quiet breathing.
Therefore, on every morrow, are we wreathing

A flowery band to bind us to the earth,
Spite of despondence, of the human dearth

Of noble natures, of the gloomy days,
Of all the unhealthy and o'er-darken'd ways

Made for our searching: yes, in spite of all,
Some shape of beauty moves away the pall

From our dark spirits. Such the sun, the moon,
Trees old and young, sprouting a shady boon

For simple sheep; and such are daffodils
With the green world they live in and clear rills

That for themselves a cooling covert make
'Gainst the hot season; the mid-forest brake,

Rich with a sprinkling of fair musk-rose blooms:
And such too is the grandeur of the dooms

We have imagined for the mighty dead;
All lovely tales that we have heard or read;

An endless fountain of immortal drink,
Pouring unto us from the heaven's brink.

John Keats

Mark Twain says...

Training is everything. The peach was once a bitter almond; cauliflower is nothing but cabbage with a college education.

As to the adjective, when in doubt, strike it out.

He was as shy as a newspaper is when referring to its own merits.

The universal brotherhood of man is our most precious possession—what there is of it.

Prosperity is the best protector of principle.

By trying we can easily learn to endure adversity. Another man's, I mean.

Everyone is a moon, and has a dark side which he never shows to anybody.

When in doubt, tell the truth.

Truth is stranger than fiction, but it is because fiction is obliged to stick to possibilities; truth isn't.

Truth is the most valuable thing we have. Let us economize it.

It is easier to stay out than get out.

Always do right. This will gratify some people, and astonish the rest.

October. This is one of the peculiarly dangerous months to speculate in stocks. The others are July, January, September, April, November, May, March, June, December, August and February.

The Bettmann Archive, Inc.

Quotations from the works of Mark Twain published by Harper & Row, Publishers, Inc. and reprinted by permission.

Things I Love

These are the things I dearly love:
The azure blue of skies above
And soft, green grass beneath my feet,
The quiet of a village street,
The smell of fresh-baked bread at noon,
The yellow glow of a harvest moon,
Two small, white kittens hard at play
And whippoorwills at close of day;
The fireflies' glow, a hoot-owl's call,
The liquid notes of a waterfall.

Little girls with wind-blown hair,
Old slippers and a comfy chair,
The silver threads among the gold,
A blazing log when nights are cold.
The sunset's gilt in summer's sky,
A mother's soft, sweet lullaby,
A friend to greet, a dog to bark,
The lights of home when streets are dark,
The cheery buzz of friendly throngs,
The clasp of hands, the old sweet songs.

Reginald Holmes

52

GENESIS

From the earth, I scooped a hollow
. . . Filled it up with water, cool . . . Birds,
like angels, gathered round me . . .
Watched me build my garden pool.

Life, by twos, I placed within it . . . in
my world of liquid space . . . Snails I
chose to do the labor . . . Fish to please
me with their grace.

Then I added swirling lilies . . .
Mossy rocks, both large and small . . .
Saw the beauty, slowly forming . . .
Pleased was I and loved it all.

With my task at last completed . . .
Down beside the pool I knelt . . . Looked
upon the life below me . . . Knew how
God, Himself, had felt.

Martin Buxbaum

Autumn

Autumn Song

In this season of garnered grain,
Russet beauty in every lane,
My heart knows peace . . . a quiet gladness . . .
A simple, timeless, sweet refrain.

Ernestine Lamont

Harvest

Mary E. Linton

Now is the harvest time, spring
    did not lie.
Ripe fruit hangs full upon the
    weighted bough,
Red, crisp and fragrant, while
    the locusts cry
Of autumn's urgency, of frost,
    "Now! Now!"

*Who guards young April's blossoms
    picks the fruit
That only summer's bounty
    can endow . . .
The slow maturing, the sun's
    pursuit,
The promised reaping . . . it is
    autumn now.*

Time proves which things are
    strong enough to last,
Which can endure through wind,
    through drought and flood,
The out-of-season cold, the
    searing blast,
To flow in rhythm with earth's
    throbbing blood.

*September days are rich and
    full with knowing . . .
What April dreamed, what summer
    spent in growing.*

©

Belief

I do not always understand
The many things I see:
The hills that climb to meet the sky,
The shore that finds the sea,
A shining star at close of day
As twilight gathers near,
And then the darkness all about
As night is quickly here.

I do not always analyze
The things before my eyes:
The mysteries too deep to know,
The hours of sweet surprise,
A stream that flows through valleys deep,
The river rushing on,
The desert sand so dry and still,
The day that's here and gone.

Belief is mine; although 'tis true
I know not how or why,
The rain shall end as it began
And sunshine light the sky.
'Tis faith alone that tells my heart
The winter too shall pass,
And spring will come to bless the world
An April day at last.

I cannot always understand
These miracles of God;
But one day all of us shall walk
The path that angels trod.
Still, I believe and always shall
In so much yet unseen;
Because a faith lives in my heart,
Belief is mine supreme.

Garnett Ann Schultz

Indian Summer

Indian summer in the forest
　Is enchantment to behold
When the birch leaves turn to yellow
　And the maple's red and gold.

The dark green of the hemlock
　And the fragrance of the pines
And errant rays of sunshine
　In long and slanting lines.

Still there is more enchantment
　In this scene with charm replete,
'Tis the whirr of feathery pinions
　And the patter of scurrying feet.

It is the little folk of the forest
　That love to romp and play,
Or store up their cache of treasure
　For a cold and wintry day,

The sudden flight of the partridge,
　The squirrels with their bushy tails,
The ever cautious rabbits
　Mapping their winter trails.

We are thankful for such beautiful scenes,
　Our hearts fill with delight,
And pleasant memories linger
　While the scene turns sparkling white.

Wenzel A. Seiler

Family Love

No love is quite as great it seems
As family love and family dreams,
A mother's smile, the tenderness
Bestowed on those she loves the best . . .
It matters not as time goes by
A love still shines within her eyes.

No other love is quite the same
As Dad's, who seeks no worldly fame,
But just his place within each heart
Where home fires glow . . . a special part,
A love to cherish, still his own,
A satisfaction yet unknown.

No other love, however real,
Can match a family love ideal,
The dreams and plans so much to each,
The worthwhile things just out of reach,
And yet it makes no difference there . . .
Where home fires burn, all life is fair.

There is no beauty quite left out
If Dad and Mom are still about,
The little ones with eyes that shine,
Their world a heaven quite divine . . .
We find that God smiles from above
Because He shares in family love.

Garnett Ann Schultz

Autumn Song

Sing a song of autumn,
  Apples sparkling bright,
Robins in the treetops
  Singing with delight.

    Sing a song of chipmunks,
      And songs of meadowlarks,
    Sing of squirrels a-chattering,
      Their tails all question marks.

        Sing a song of schooltimes,
          With books to read again,
        Games and sports and skipping,
          And cleansing autumn rain.

        Sing of homes and families,
          Of relatives and friends,
        Sing of autumn's beauty
          And all the love God sends.

Lola Sneyd

It's Halloween Again

Halloween is here again
With golden pumpkins all about;
Goblins now will come a-spying,
Witches through the air a-flying,
Funny faces we'll be buying;
At dark of night we'll all go out.

Halloween is here again . . .
Autumn leaves come tumbling down,
Black cats will slink about tonight,
The moon will shed an eerie light;
"Trick or treat" will bring delight
From every house in town.

We all look forward to the time
When Halloween is here,
Owls will hoot high in the trees
And we will brave the chilly breeze
That heralds winter's coming freeze . . .
October's time of year.

So join me on this special night
When ghostlike shapes are seen;
We'll duck for apples, spin the pan,
Play blindman's buff and tag our man,
Pull taffy, fragrant, golden tan . . .
This night of Halloween.

Eleanor Elkins

There is one pleasure
I like to recall . . .
Bobbing for apples,
How that amused one and all!
We were bound and determined
Into the apples to bite,
As they kept floating around
To everyone's delight.

In a huge wooden bucket
The apples would bob
As we filled it with water
Clear up to the top;
And many a time
A dousing we'd get,
While some happy prankster
Would shout "Let's get wet!"
And push our eager faces
Deep down in the tub,
We'd come up gasping,
Not expecting that dub!

Bobbing for Apples

On through the years
This sport can be seen,
On the festive occasion
Of each Halloween.
A faint wisp of smile
Comes o'er my face,
As I muse for a moment
How I tried to embrace
A floating red apple
Between my set teeth,
But somehow or other
I never accomplished that feat.

Ann Schneider

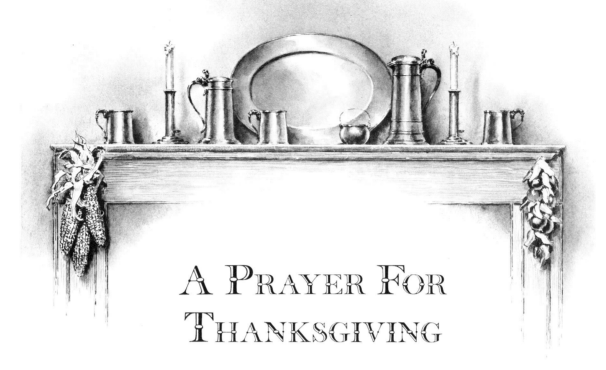

A Prayer For Thanksgiving

Lord, bless the bounties of this table
And the length that it extends,
Making room for all the children,
Plus the neighbors and our friends.

Bless the beauty of the springtime
And the heat of harvest day,
Bringing crops to feed the family
And enough to store away.

Bless the cozy home that holds us
Through the rains and winter storm
With a fireplace that's glowing
And the wood to keep us warm.

Bless the health that gives us courage
For the tasks we have to do,
And the power to enjoy it
When a hard days work is through.

Make us grateful for the little things
That chance to pass our way,
Making life seem extra special,
When comes Thanksgiving Day.

Harriet Feltham

Autumn Hills at Dusk

With dignity each ancient temple stands
Secure and rugged, clad in vine, with glow
Of sumac's crimson lanterns burning low
While healing dusk replies to day's demands.

As if they were an ancient sexton's hands,
The fox grapes swing their bell ropes to and fro;
There will be deeper silences of snow
Across these russet hills and valley lands.

The silence steals across the land unseen
When brilliant autumn touches leaf and flower
And sumac bobs light up these ancient hills.

Here is a quiet, tranquil and serene,
A glory garlanding the passing hour
When autumn dusk comes healing earthly ills.

Ethel Green Russell

The Voice

A little log house by the side of the road
Seems to speak to me
Of folks it sheltered long ago;
I can almost see
The hands that fashioned rough-hewn beams,
The chimney of clay and stone,
The blackened hearth that held bright flames
For women who waited there.

Vines have covered the sagging roof,
Wild roses crowd the door,
A bird's nest clings to the windowsill,
Chipmunks dart under the floor.
I lift the latch and step inside . . .
In the quiet here
The echo of faith speaks to my heart . . .
The voice of the pioneer.

Ethel Hopper

Many times we've reaped and gathered the glowing harvest yield . . . the burnished fruit and orange pumpkins . . . the yellow gold of ripened fields . . . We've thrilled to see the corn in tassel and the heavy apple boughs . . . and stood in grateful silence beneath a bulging mow.

Many times we've strolled where red and gold still lingered on the hill . . . where acorns crunched beneath our feet . . . and flaming trees stood silent, still . . . Many times we've found a quiet place to reap the blessings of the year . . . to gather in the warmth of smiles . . . the thoughtful words and moments dear . . . A quiet place where we could dream of fruitful deeds that mellowed long . . . of seeds of kindness that were sown . . . that blossomed into grateful song.

Many times we've lingered there alone, from all the world apart . . . to thank God for His love and care . . . and reap the treasures of the heart.

Joy Belle Burgess

To Autumn

Season of mists and mellow fruitfulness!
  Close bosom-friend of the maturing sun;
Conspiring with him how to load and bless
  With fruit the vines that round the thatch-eave run;
To bend with apples the moss'd cottage-trees,
  And fill all fruit with ripeness to the core;
To swell the gourd, and plump the hazel shells
With a sweet kernel; to set budding more,
And still more, later flowers for the bees,
Until they think warm days will never cease,
  For Summer has o'er-brimm'd their clammy cells.

Where are the songs of Spring? Ay, where are they?
  Think not of them, thou hast thy music too—
While barred clouds bloom the soft-dying day,
  And touch the stubble plains with rosy hue;
Then in a wailful choir the small gnats mourn
  Among the river swallows, borne aloft
  Or sinking as the light wind lives or dies;
And full-grown lambs loud bleat from hilly bourn;
  Hedge-crickets sing; and now with treble soft
  The redbreast whistles from a garden croft;
  And gathering swallows twitter in the skies.

John Keats

78

Trees have a way of talking to us—oh, not in so many words. But they tell us things just the same—if we listen and observe and are still. A forest can be both cathedral and classroom to the receptive, and a single tree can furnish enough food for thought for the lifetime of man.

Esther Baldwin York

I traveled a land of painted trees,
    colored by autumn's hand,
On a carpet of gold, of russet and
    brown which covered the forest
    land.
I gathered the leaves which fell at my
    feet and tossed them into the sun,
And watched them float in the gentle
    breeze, seemingly full of fun.
I stopped and gazed at the blue of the
    skies through pillars of golden
    hue,
And noted approaching ships of the
    air reflecting the gold in the blue.
It was peaceful and calm in this silent
    lane where the carol of autumn
    was played.
And my heart sang out with thanks
    to God for this land which His
    hand had made.

Everett Wentworth Hill

Slow Me Down, Lord

Slow me down, Lord! Ease the pounding of my heart by the quieting of my mind. Steady my hurried pace with a vision of the eternal reach of time.

Give me, amid the confusion of my day, the calm of the everlasting hills. Break the tensions of my nerves and muscles with the music of the singing streams that live in my memory.

Help me to know the magical restoring power of sleep.

Teach me the art of taking minute vacations: of slowing down to look at a flower, to chat with a friend, to pat a dog, to read a few lines from a good book.

Remind me each day of the fable of the hare and the tortoise that I may know that the race is not always to the swift; that there is more to life than increasing its speed.

Let me look upward into the branches of the towering oak and know that it grew great and strong because it grew slowly and well. Slow me down, Lord, and inspire me to send my roots deep into the soil of life's enduring values that I may grow toward the stars of my greater destiny. Amen.

Wilferd A. Peterson

Winter

Another Sweet December

Ben Burroughs

December is a happy month . . . Of peace and real good will . . . The grand finale of our climb . . . Across another hill . . . The prelude to a brand new year . . . And all that it will bring . . . December is a joyful month . . . To which we tightly cling . . . For near its end we celebrate . . . The greatest day of all . . . Christmas with its carols and its evergreens so tall . . . December is the children's month . . . When youth runs on a spree . . . Waiting on old Santa Claus to fill their hearts with glee . . . December welcomes wintertime and dreams of long ago . . . Yes, somehow every time it comes . . . Deep down inside I glow . . . Because it weaves a mellow web of times that I remember . . . Thank God that I'm alive to see . . . Another sweet December.

Postscript

One frosty New Year's morning,
　A stranger gave to me
A branch still green and tinselled
　From some old Christmas tree.
And when I would have spoken,
　"You think of it," said he.

At first I felt bewildered.
　I could not understand
This sudden gift of balsam
　Now in my mittened hand.
And then I saw the forest
　And sensed the hidden land.

I stood inside a clearing
　Where once a tree had grown.
The snow was melting strongly,
　I did not seem alone
And on the ground before me
　There lay a single cone.

Elisabeth W. Morss

Snow Silence

When pine trees stand in falling snow that whirs,
　The earth is taut and somber, each trunk-stalk
Is buried under frost of prickly burrs;
　There is no verdant green to trim the walk.

　　Winter winds are blustery; the cold is tense,
　　　The swallows have departed; nothing grows.
　　The hive is still and silent, the creaking fence,
　　　The russet woods are white with heavy snows.

　　　　A sense of static wonder transcends fear;
　　　　　Above the buried roots, the air is sweet.
　　　　Within the thick-leaved branches, far and near,
　　　　　The birds in hurried throngs have formed retreat.

D. M. Pettinella

Christmastime is Here

Hearts are filled with laughter
And everybody's gay,
Passersby all greet you
In a warm and friendly way.

There's the greatest kind of feeling,
One that fills the heart with cheer
And lingers like a sweet refrain,
For Christmastime is here.

Lights are shining softly
Through windows sparkling bright;
Snow, like purest ermine,
Has dressed the world in white.

There's the greatest kind of feeling
Lingering round this time of year,
Making everybody happy
For Christmastime is here.

Carolers are singing
The Christmas carols sweet,
And the season's best of wishes
Are exchanged by all who meet.

Bells high in the steeple
Ring out in tones so clear,
Today was born a Saviour
And Christmastime is here.

Mrs. Paul E. King

ow when Jesus was born in Bethlehem of Judea in the days of Herod the king, behold, there came wise men from the east to Jerusalem.

Saying, Where is he that is born King of the Jews? for we have seen his star in the east, and are come to worship him.

When Herod the king had heard these things, he was troubled, and all Jerusalem with him.

And when he had gathered all the chief priests and scribes of the people together, he demanded of them where Christ should be born.

And they said unto him, In Bethlehem of Judea: for thus it is written by the prophet,

And thou Bethlehem, in the land of Juda, art not the least among the princes of Juda: for out of thee shall come a Governor, that shall rule my people Israel.

Then Herod, when he had privily called the wise men, enquired of them diligently what time the star appeared.

And he sent them to Bethlehem, and said, Go and search diligently for the young child; and when ye have found him, bring me word again, that I may come and worship him also.

When they had heard the king, they departed; and, lo, the star, which they saw in the east, went before them, till it came and stood over where the young child was.

When they saw the star, they rejoiced with exceeding great joy.

And when they were come into the house, they saw the young child with Mary his mother, and fell down, and worshipped him: and when they had opened their treasures, they presented unto him gifts; gold, and frankincense, and myrrh.

And being warned of God in a dream that they should not return to Herod, they departed into their own country another way.

Matthew 2:1-12

Music

Mary Stoner Wine

I love to hear a sweet familiar song
With even cadence, soft and clear and low,
A singing melody that lingers long
And fills my memory with its rhythmic flow.

I love to hear romantic sweet old songs
That lovers' lips have whispered long ago,
For such a song to youth and age belongs
With mingled hope and memory's sacred glow.

I love a cradle song. The mother's eyes
And voice sing with their lovelit charms.
'Tis then I think of Mary's lullabies
When Jesus was a baby in her arms.

I love the lifting worship of a hymn
When voices, blended with the organ's tone,
Ascend in great harmonic chords to Him
Until earth's anthems echo round God's throne.

I love the minor music, strains of joy,
Clear voices mingled with the reeds and strings,
Sweet melodies mere words cannot employ,
The paeans lifting deep desires on wings.

©

THE STORY OF SANTA CLAUS

Once upon a time, a man called Nicholas lived in Patara, a town in the East. Because he was very fond of children and was kind and generous to them, they came to think of him as their dear friend and their beloved saint. So it was that after a time the wonderful things he did were woven into a beautiful legend. You know that *Santa* means *Saint* and *Claus* stands for *Nicholas,* and that is how he came to be known as Santa Claus.

In Santa Claus's own town, Patara, lived a great lord who had three daughters. He was very poor, so poor that one day he was on the point of sending his daughters out to beg for food from his neighbors. But it happened that Saint Nicholas not long before had come into a fortune, and as he loved giving to those in need, he no sooner heard of the trouble the poor lord was in than he made up his mind to help him secretly. So he went to the nobleman's house at night, and as the moon shone out from behind a cloud, he saw an open window into which he threw a bag of gold, and with this timely gift the father was able to provide for his eldest daughter, so that she could be married. On another night Santa Claus set off with another bag of gold, and threw it in at the window, so the second daughter was provided for. But by this time, the father had grown eager to discover who the mysterious visitor could be, and next night he kept on the lookout. Then for the third time Santa Claus came with a bag of gold upon his back and pitched it in at the window. The old lord at once recognized his fellow townsman, and falling on his knees, cried out: "Oh! Nicholas, servant of God, why seek to hide yourself?"

Is it not wonderful to think that this was so long ago, sixteen hundred years, yet we still look for the secret coming of Santa Claus with his Christmas gifts? At first he was said to come on his own birthday, which is early in December, but after awhile, as was very natural with Christmas so near, the night of his coming was moved on in the calendar, and now we hang up our stockings to receive his gifts on Christmas Eve. In some countries children still put their shoes by the fireside on his birthday. In others they say it is the Christ-Kindlein or Christ Child who brings the gifts at Christmastime. But it is always a surprise visit, and though it has happened so many hundreds of times, the hanging up of the Christmas stocking is still as great a delight as ever.

Author Unknown

The Magic of Christmas

The magic of Christmas
    Is tied in each bow;
It glistens and sparkles
    In new-fallen snow.
It rings in the tolling
    Of silvery bells
And lingers unending
    In savory smells.

The magic of Christmas
    Hangs in each wreath;
It mingles and harkens
    The very word "peace."
It's wrapped up in packages
    Cheerful and gay;
And lies in a stable
    With a Babe in the hay.

The magic of Christmas
    Is hung on a tree
And peers from the face
    Of an angel I see.
It smiles on a child
    Almost bursting with joy
And glows in the eyes
    Of each girl and boy.

Ruth H. Underhill

Christmas Gifts

Some packages are lovely
    With fancy bow and tie;
The paper looks so glossy
    It captivates the eye.

It's not the pretty ribbon
    Or cover bright and bold,
But the spirit of the giver
    Hidden in the fold.

Wrap a little of yourself
    And tie it with a smile,
Fill it full of warmth and love
    And give a gift worthwhile!

Betty Cooke

98

Come...Christmas Morning

Alice Leedy Mason

The attic holds treasures,
   Outmoded of course,
Two clowns on a pull toy,
   Tin soldiers . . . a horse.

An old-fashioned doll
   With a trunkful of clothes,
A stove with an oven,
   A machine that still sews.

A game and some blocks,
   A car built to last,
And other quaint relics
   Of the memorable past . . .

While nestled close-by,
   So pleasant to see,
Are gifts that are waiting
   To be placed neath the tree.

No clue to their contents,
   No hint of the toys,
Just presents awaiting
   Good girls and boys.

The attic holds treasures
   Hidden snug from the weather,
The past and the future
   Are waiting together.

The thought comes to mind
   As they wait Christmas Day . . .
Will the new toys be loved
   In the old-fashioned way?

Christmas

Patricia Clafford

Christmas is a time of faith,
a faith engendering joyous love.
Christmas is love.

Christmas is the illuminating
star of all the world . . . a power
that lights the way with the
holy message of the nativity story.
Christmas is the light.

Christmas is a time for music . . .
of psalms, sung with heaven's
words, and caroling miraculous works . . .
the essenced song of songs.
Christmas is a song.

Christmas is the vibrancy and
color embodying all time and
all space . . . rainbowing in our
world, as the bow that shines
in the clouds.
Christmas is a rainbow.

Christmas is a time to expand
our giving, encompassing the
friendless and needy . . . near and far.
Christmas is sharing.

Christmas is a time to forget
our inhibitions, to tread mentally
in our brother's shoes.
Christmas is brotherhood.

Christmas is a time when man's
heart unfolds with the manna and
the leaven of hope, as he sees the
love and confidence of a child, even
as it has been said, "A little child
shall lead them."
Christmas is the Child.

Christmas is that little time
when with all honor and splendor
we commemorate the birth of the
Saviour of the world, our spirit
soaring in renewal. It is the
embracement of all the glory
that is and ever shall be, whose
majesty and effulgence haloes
every age.
Christmas is life's refreshment.

©

For unto us a child is born, unto us a son is given: and the government shall be upon his shoulder: and his name shall be called Wonderful, Counsellor, The mighty God, The everlasting Father, The Prince of Peace. Of the increase of his government and peace there shall be no end, upon the throne of David, and upon his kingdom, to order it, and to establish it with judgment and with justice from henceforth even for ever.

Isaiah 9:6, 7

PAUL
MANN

The First Snow

Robert Freeman Bound

We waited for hours,
As children all will,
After Father had told us
The news with a thrill:

'Twas the oddest sensation
When we'd gaze at the sky;
We seemed to be falling,
But we didn't know why.

Next morning the light
Reflected from snow
Made shimmering patterns
With walls all aglow;

From lowering clouds
And a temperature fall,
The first snow of winter
Would come with a squall.

Then early that evening
The first flakes descended;
And when we retired
The fall hadn't ended.

We looked from our beds
At a white, silent scene
Of tall, pearly trees
And the buildings between.

And our happy, old dog,
With great barking leaps,
Was chasing a rabbit
Through high, snowy heaps.

Oh, the wonderful joy
To be young and know
The thrill of a child
At winter's first snow.

Christmas Music

Bernard L. Boss

The miraculous power of music,
According to legend of old,
Has always enraptured the people,
The young, as well as the old.

How dear are the memories that linger
Of the first songs that entered our heart
When in a youth service at Christmas
We began to take a real part

In singing those beautiful carols
Of our Saviour, the newborn King,
To whom even the oldest of wise men
From afar their presents did bring.

There never was a greater blessing
Bestowed on God's people on earth
Than the charm of those beautiful carols
Composed to honor Christ's birth.

Now again church choirs at Christmas
Their peace message carry afar
As once did the choirs of angels
Beneath that bright guiding star.

When in the right spirit we listen
To the "Messiah" and "Silent Night,"
We cannot but say, "There is music!
Which really is art at its height,

Where orchestra, voice and the organ
So advantageously may be employed
That actually a part of real heaven
Can down here on earth be enjoyed."

Thank God for this beautiful music
Which plays such a dominant part
In bringing the sweet Christmas message
Of peace and good will to our heart.

©

Winter Woods

Winter woods aren't desolate
As they would seem to be,
For beauty dwells at every turn
For searching eyes to see.

The black of trees is ermine trimmed;
Each bush is wearing lace,
And Nature's spread with lavish hand
White velvet every place.

Where winter sunrays lightly touch
The ice-encrusted stream,
Upon its crystal countenance
A thousand diamonds gleam.

No, winter woods aren't desolate—
There's beauty enough to spare;
And those in search of loveliness
Will surely find it there.

Virginia Blanck Moore

The World Has Need of You

Evelyn Whitell

If it's ever so small the part you take,
　　The world has need of you.
Be it big or little the effort you make,
　　The world has need of you.
If it's only a thought you give by the way,
If it's only love's word you pause to say,
It's a part that nobody else can play,
　　So the world has need of you.

By your smile you can change another's life;
　　The world has need of you.
By a word you can bring peace out of strife;
　　The world has need of you.
Then lift your head and never say die;
Count every blessing, stop every sigh.
Get busy . . . don't let a chance slip by,
　　For the world has need of you.

*Our sincere thanks to the author
whose address we were unable to locate*

ACKNOWLEDGMENTS

FROM NAZARETH HE COMES by Raymond Kresenky. Copyright Christian Century Foundation. Reprinted by permission from THE CHRISTIAN CENTURY. SLOW ME DOWN, LORD by Wilferd A. Peterson. Copyrighted. Used with permission of the author. A CHILD IS SOMEONE TO LOVE by Berna Rauch. Reprinted courtesy GIRL TALK Magazine. Copyright 1973. Our sincere thanks to the following authors whose addresses we were unable to locate: Mary Carolyn Davies for THE SUNSHINE SHOP; Olive Lair Smith for LAUGHTER.